G000155578

# BROKEN SLEEP

**Sally Read**'s first book of poems, *The Point of Splitting* (Bloodaxe Books 2005) was shortlisted for the Jerwood Aldeburgh prize for best first collection. *Broken Sleep* (Bloodaxe Books, 2009) is her second collection.

In 2001 she received an Eric Gregory Award. She is a teacher of English and creative writing, and was formerly a psychiatric nurse. Married with a daughter, she lives between Bungay, Suffolk and Santa Marinella, Rome.

# SALLY READ

# BROKEN SLEEP

BLOODAXE BOOKS

Copyright © Sally Read 2009

ISBN: 978 1 85224 845 1

First published 2009 by
Bloodaxe Books Ltd,
Highgreen,
Tarset,
Northumberland NE48 1RP.

www.bloodaxebooks.com
For further information about Bloodaxe titles
please visit our website or write to
the above address for a catalogue.

Bloodaxe Books Ltd acknowledges
the financial assistance of
Arts Council England, North East.

LEGAL NOTICE

All rights reserved. No part of this book may be
reproduced, stored in a retrieval system, or
transmitted in any form, or by any means, electronic,
mechanical, photocopying, recording or otherwise,
without prior written permission from Bloodaxe Books Ltd.

Requests to publish work from this book
must be sent to Bloodaxe Books Ltd.

Sally Read has asserted her right under
Section 77 of the Copyright, Designs and Patents Act 1988
to be identified as the author of this work.

Cover design: Neil Astley & Pamela Robertson-Pearce.

Printed in Great Britain by
Bell & Bain Limited, Glasgow, Scotland.

*For Celia*

# ACKNOWLEDGEMENTS

Thanks are due to the editors of the following publications in which some of these poems, occasionally in a different form, first appeared: *Dreamcatcher, Eyewear, Lifelines* (Poets for Oxfam CD), *Litro, Magma, The Manhattan Review, Notes from the Underground, Nth Position, Pagine* and *The Wolf*. 'Mafia Flowers' won second prize in the 2005 Strokestown poetry competition.

Warmest thanks to Gregory Leadbetter, Lawrence Sail, Joanna Solfrian and Baron Wormser for advice and support; to Candy Hamilton for so patiently and expertly answering my endless questions about recent American-Indian history, and for taking me to Anna Mae Pictou-Aquash's grave; and to Kerry Lee Crabbe for everything, always.

# CONTENTS

# I

## BROKEN SLEEP

We shall not cease from exploration
And the end of all our exploring
Will be to arrive where we started
And know the place for the first time.

T.S. ELIOT

# The Crossing

The night we left the island for good
I woke six hours from port
to the engine's buoyant throb,
cabin so black I couldn't know
my open eyes from closed.

The sea tilted, and every organ
in its liquid capsule rocked.
Salt and diesel, the queasy fuel.
That day, I understood that you
had taken root, and the image

of what you would become
was an unpickable fabric
of skin: elbows tucked, head
bent as if breasting wind. Night
and water unwound for hours.

You were a blue cross on white,
so small you'd shrivel on
the minerals of my palm. Nothing
in your history will tell you this,
nor mimic this remote

embedding, the intimate
loneliness. At 3 A.M.
the way back is equidistant
to the way forward; longer
than an outstretched arm.

# Hyacinths

It was a rite,
to pack the bulbs in peat

and hide them in the certain
darkness

of a wardrobe
among clean towels

and naked pipes,
the unstable forest of clothes

above. It had all
the pointlessness of early

schooling (cloves shoved
into oranges,

cress sprinkled
on wet cotton-wool).

But as you begin
to swim within me,

I think again
of the hyacinths' black closet:

the plumbing's amplified drip
and squall;

an occasional disembodied
voice as my mother

put away the sheets
(calling, sighing,

like the rumour of a god);
an immaculate

solitude as strata of vegetable
skin on skin was laid.

Is this dark gestation
what it is to be held?

Or does the foetus ache
in its seclusion,

and crave a mother's
hands?

Even the most chaste
and isolated saint

(Saint Francis in his
earthen cell;

Saint Cecilia entrusting
her stiffly

guarded virginity
to the angel)

has sunlight and dirty
glitter imprinted

on the eyes; flesh
that remembers touch.

(All bodies,
however long alone,

must sing with this.)
As kids we forgot

the hyacinths.
We never reckoned

the hive of cells
we'd set in train as we biked

around the winter garden.
You are like

those nascent flowers,
gearing up to loose

their endless scent.
You are what every saint

must long to be:
craning whitely,

loved and absolutely
untouched,

to some unimaginable
point of light.

# Hearing the Heart

The light of the ultrasound room
is a train station at night: incisive
neon, cold shafts of grey-green,
the sense of a stopping place
in the face of a larger shifting,
like a country station with its two
tracks funnelling all the chilled air
of the Fens, and without warning,
the peremptory heart is the slamming
of the non-stop train that won't wait
for boarding, its size beyond us,
our edges splayed by the force,
and each length slinging an agenda
to charge the passing; each beat
a window, the systole a slim
prophecy of silence, cancelled
in less than a thought by diastole,
the piston's tight inevitability.
The body can't comprehend
limitlessness. Or how, in the night's
hollow, I know your rangy futures
unfurling independent of me.
This is how we stand, your parents:
bystanders, pressed a fraction
more featureless by the suddenly
displaced air. And, as the probe lifts
from my pelvis, there's a new listening
implanted in us – to what continues
to pass, elsewhere.

## On the Beach

The sea is white as the sky, thick as single cream.
Three boatmen pierce it with pikes, plunge deep
to grind out a shallow passage. Nothing else
but a salty hiss, the tissue of absence,

when you float blindly, and break for the first
time, light as a bubble, on my flesh. My pelvis
sucks itself in, waits so long you swallow
your own happening, only to half-beat again.

The boatmen's voices skim like pebbles.
They work the sea's back, wrapped in white.
I know you now: exquisitely grazed, listening
as the water stipples to insects, the faintest rain.

# June Evening

Jasmine sweats an odour
far-flung as the hormones
of libidinous cats. Its wax-
white emanates too, a lit
skin long beyond itself.
There's live jazz down
the street: the laryngeal
moan of a saxophone;
a beat trembling
in the dark polish
of leaves. These days
your sparrow-bones
are vivified by decibels;
a note can animate
your limbs like fear.
I'm seduced by your mute
exposure to the world.
Your jelly transparency
colours with all my flooding
chemistry (a starburst
of adrenaline, the subtle
tide of melatonin now).
You're the pure narcissus
I used to arrange in a glass
of cochineal – to despoil,
to harness their delicate veins.

# The Belly

Six months gone, a succession
of diamonds crazes my navel:
each growth-spurt snagging
its mark, like the rings of a tree.

Your father enfolds me from behind,
*I would have you always like this.*
When his fingers trace the bump's
topography of silver rivulets

you thrash and fling yourself up
like a muscular fish. And his face –
a man whose hand falls through glass
as he reaches into a mirror.

# Gestation

Through flesh, muscle, water your hand
nudges my hand – recoils. Ticking over
in salt-water, you heal. Then your arm
extends, meets my palm – you lean on me:
shy, listening. Alluvium of churned
fluid, settling
               and I think of the fumy
stomach of our old pond, how the bottled
light of Koi rose, let me tickle their cilia
fins, the clitoral stem beneath. I wanted
them lumped in my cupped hands, to coax
down a shiny, bumping heart the way
I'd stroke a tablet down the dry throat
of a dog. They were lethal: eyes
and scales wild as head-lights; confusion
of fish-flesh, and sunless reflection.
I did ram a hand wrist-deep (into water
so bitter it numbed the bones), and they
subsided from sight, stunned and hurt.
Night drained the garden. I was called in
to the meaty steam of dinner, windows
solidifying against the pond until I couldn't
see it and forgot,
                  but in the pond's agitation
the fish soothed, lifted with a bovine,
unthinking grace, like difficult memories –
that tremendous, unstoppable blossoming.

## Through Glass

When you come,
the oranges will be done.

Cold's cured
the green skins bright.

The leaves are glossier
than this night,

dense as bone,
and segments sustain,

ready to tear
with a white, bated sound.

This winter I watch them
through glass,

every hour struggling
to my feet.

You slip, scrabble
to your own position.

On my feet we limp,
reshuffle,

placid as Siamese twins.
Your skull

hums on my bladder
as I pee;

you trill one slithery
foot to my rib.

I can hardly contain you.
But I'm rubber-tight,

tough and unlikely
as an eyeball to split.

When you come,
the oranges will be soft,

the last cricket
that shocks the pine

with its lacquered ring
will be picked off,

and together we'll hear
the amber pockets

of the last train melt
to one.

Back in my seat,
I would keep this flawless

world still. At 4 A.M. the rain
issues whole,

dies the second after
its shattering swell,

as though it were cast
out of the sky complete.

# The Waiting

You quietened when they held your face to mine,
as though you'd entered a house, out of the wind.
Your scrunched eyes waxed to black,
did the telescopic slide as you took me in.
My arms were dead so it was left to them
to rub your cheek to mine, and back again.
Then they took you away to scream.
Two hours of waiting. They tugged up the skin
of my legs to mend the rent you made;

wheeled me to a room on my own, my thoughts
lobbed off by morphine, my body half-gone.
I want you to know I was an amnesiac
in those hours. My old life was yesterday's
clothes: ill-fitting, redundant with blood.
My sappy nerves revved under the weight
of dead legs, but there was no beginning.
I waited without expectation or any way out,
as though I waited for my own name.

## Latching On

Your head's cloaked in my bath-robe
as you jut my breast, frantic to dock.
In the gaunt light of late night TV
you beat me with your fists and shriek
for milk.
            I strip us both, lie giant
on the bed and set you on my stomach
where you clamber, eyes bigger
and exhausted with knowledge.
You root my belly, ribs, even
the clavicle's hard edge,
but when you find a nipple
you take the breast in adult,
outstretched hands, your lower lip
splays, toothless gums sink
into me, and the rhythmic suck
draws us flush. Then a rusty
connection from nipple to uterus
tautens, and my innards shirr
on an ancient wire.
                And the way
you look at me, as the drink gathers
its gulping momentum, has a religious
stillness. It sees, soberly, past all
my fragile edges. Like a lover's eyes.
Or rather, a lover's like yours.

# The Lullaby Hours

We swing from window
to wardrobe, to flying
pink teddies above the crib
as she clings to my shoulder

in her green sleep. Since
the raw lights of birth
dragged her from dark
muck to brute cleanliness

she's ignited with wakefulness,
and it won't let her be.
She gnaws fists, bangs
her head at my neck,

and if she relaxes,
like a drowsy driver
on a long road trip,
the startle reflex pricks,

starring her hands.
You only need sing.
All night if need be.
And move, keep mooching

with no glitch of stasis.
Then her fingers
splay like pond-weed
and the small skull gives

an inch. We chip away
at the daylight. We swing
metronomically. I sing
*Moon River* so low

just vowels emerge,
and she glances sleep
as a crane-fly glances
water. It is all faith,

as she lets go finger by
finger, till the roly limbs
hang against me in mock
death. I erase sounds

at each verse, as with
each revolution we creep
to the cot. I guess now,
as fists unclench,

and the face fattens
(glutted on trust),
she's back where she began.
I bear her up:

nightie and cheek
are fossil-flat, etched
with creases. Her hands,
still upraised, push

fervently on nothing.
I give her to gravity
as slow as I can,
and my lips keep
on singing –

## Broken Sleep

I wake to a residue of milk
playing in your throat.
Through the window starlings
coagulate in the no-colour dawn,

each bird distinct, but utterly
in thrall to formations of twist,
kite, looming bee-swarm.
Your single cry's answered

by a parched breaking in my chest
and a laboured rush
of hot liquid. As I lift you
from your crib, still balled up

and loaded with sleep, I know
soon you'll uncurl, walk away
to a point I can't hear you.
The birds rise together as though

on an up-draught. I spread
your outstretched fingers
on the back of my hand as you
work away at one breast –

ears pulling in time, toes curling;
your whole body drinking –
and lost milk from my other breast
grows cold as rain on my nightdress.

# Entrenched

You howl so loud my feet tattoo the stairs,
and you're a-brim with wet, red sorrow, eyes
seared shut with hurt. I fit your face to mine
(you heave down as a sailor does on terra firma),
and breathe it in: the scent of dogs careering
through marshland, dried biscuity by hearth,
and some dangerous tang like short-circuited
electrics – your usual smell broken open
by distress, the way a garden's grass and rose
smells release after a battering of rain.
*I could eat you* and I do salivate, richly,
and milk bunches at my nipples, so I see
myself as blooming in fast forward – Daphne
sprouting branches, leaves from wayward
arms and hair, as she tunnels roots into her forest,
(contains the ants, the worms, independent
fecund shoots), stands lattice-fast, and rocks.

# Fog

On the slung ropes of sail-boats
fog succumbs to globules, teeters
along a helm. Here there's no
winter, just white days. Ships,
skirting the harbour, steady
with panic-filled lights.
My daughter's a stunned weight
on my shoulder, bouncing
a complacent second after
each tread. Now we are two.
The scar purses to a thin
brown line. The uterus shrinks.
But these damp days –
the same way old sailors
complain of the screws
in their knees – there's a bright
snaggle of pain, as if something
were left inside. And she observes
blandly the splintered jetty
strutting off into nothing, as though
she weren't quite here still.
As though she observed it all
in rapt safety, from an attic window.

# Orange Blossom

The alleys are constricted
with this dark slippage:

creamy pustules
that threaten to burst

like the nettle-nectar
we dared each other

to suck in the school-yard's
forbidden ditches.

Bulbs cluster, force
a close unburdening.

They hoard what mean
light they have like children

secreting a boiled sweet
in the pouring

pockets of their cheeks.
No other smell

is so complete.
It doesn't gush

from individual mouths,
like roses, stargazers.

It comes from everywhere,
and kids us that it

itself is the air,
and sweet as mother's milk.

It stalks us, has us
turn halfway down a street

as though we realised
a song we knew was playing

distantly and half-done.
It seeps, honey-thick,

through all the imperceptible
cracks of eyes, teeth,

the whole draughty
skull. It gives off,

level, unhurried,
like a slow release drug.

It is as big as the sea,
but still I unhitch you

from the pushchair,
reach you to the near-black

leaves – *Smell!*
the way the midwife

suspended you above me
and you trailed

your face so thoroughly
over mine.

## Seated

At seven months you sit on cold tiles
and don't keel over. You've found
the ground like a sail-boat at low tide,
dragged to mudflats. You're puzzled;

a sailor stepping onto a dock, dizzy
but met by land's intransigence. Your arms
and smile wave to me, the room's tipped
the right way up, and nothing gives.

Your bones know shunting now,
the finite pile-up of sensation on
sensation. You chuck your rattle down,
sombrely note that staccato *clack*.

You begin to know the lust for water,
how it fractures objects, warps, but holds.
Your arms implore me, *Mama!* and I sweep
you onto the ballast of my shoulder.

# The Note

Fork clanks on plate, pages shush.
In the distant strata of traffic I pick
out your cry with the painful precision
of a tuning fork's 'A' that skews
all other notes duff.
      It isn't you.
But as I resume fork on plate,
the turn of the page, that prospect
sustains – in a dove's putter,
the dishwasher's occasional mew –
         your note
humming at the weakest meet
of my chest, like the tuning fork's
vibration kept in readiness
for a touch – to birth
the reckoning pitch.

# Peony

The room dim behind fly-screens.
Cicadas ratcheting their waves of itch,
scratch, itch. Your face is swollen
like an unsprung peony. Asleep

on my arm it bobs and tinkers
gravity like a bud barely able
to support its neck in a glass jar.
Even in this heat your skin

is smooth. It has a dull light,
and your lashes score your cheeks,
your face so full your eye-lids
belie their sockets. You slide

between my arms, your parted lips
hovering at my breast's tip.
Dry thrill. Your mouth smacks
and dreams of milk. I think

of the five peonies I kept on my desk
last year and how I yearned
to bin them when they broke
their rash of swiftly browning secrets.

I couldn't stand the recklessness;
the deep pink and the fancy layers;
the exhaustion of promise – blasé
as the neck of a woman out of love.

# The Stranger

Iron gates harden out of darkness
and through them a little
Italian girl at a table is drawing.
She doesn't look up. She bends
and angles her body at the page
as though she's carving.

On the khaki walls, geckos spurt;
freeze. A villa's
jumpy in the dusk. Hydrangeas
give the only light: lip-pink,
bleached, with the lumpy
craters of a virus. They escape
from their pots, floaty as eye-motes,
but carnal, keen.

You toddle from my hand
and grip the gates, but the girl
doesn't look up. Instead
I show you, *Flowers*
in a language you've known
as your ears formed. Words
melded into hammer,
anvil, stirrup as new gold is melted
on a ring, or the way this clogged
twilight takes

the particularity of palm leaves,
the faint vein of pencil on a page.
*Fiori*, I could say, in the language
you'll grow in. Words
so strange to me they'll seem
to animate your tongue with
a different blood.

The little girl's intent; forgotten.
Trees roof the garden;
long doors behind her open

onto a black so matt the pupil
would gape and pound.
The hydrangeas are big as your head.
They almost rear up out
of the dark globe: fingertips
pressed bloodless to glass.

# The Supplicant

At the piano, you on my lap, I play
*Chopsticks*, *The Entertainer*, and then
you reach for the keys, warily,
as if they were alive, your fingers so light,
they only yield the wheeze of pressing,
some tinkering in the mechanism.

Then you push harder: the hammer approaches
its string. Your avid little fingers
are almost beating now (though tense
with reverence); they sound like footsteps
in a hallway. And the untapped notes
leak music as though they want to meet you;

they swarm like wind, voices,
in the darkness of a closed cathedral.

# Toddler

Tonight you're asleep before I can
get your nightie on, your head on my arm,
your half-nude body draped across
my lap. Your thighs are bloomers,
luxurious segments tapering
to round, capable calves, and hanging,
unshod feet, and so still,
                              but hissing
life in their very heat and weight,
that I think of new-shot pheasant
in the gentle mouths of dogs –
the autumnal, plump silkiness
of throat and chest feathers; the busy
brush and fretwork of red, petrol,
brown, that seems liquid, on
the brink of running. The collapsible
machinery of flight held heavy
in the eye.

# Weaning

Till now, I never told you *I love you.*
I've sat at the edge of my seat for months,
as though under questioning,
your warm body on me like an extra
roll of flesh. The wind is down,
the hearth swept out, and daylight
shows its harsh whitewash, the scab
of charred chimney.

I sit back, thin. I try to drink a whole
mug of tea. At times my breasts,
like breaking sweat, seem to fill
with milk. But they're light, so light
the emptiness knuckles on my chest.
Outside, the streets are odourless,
every sugar-filled bloom brown,
blown, gone. Now you run

the concrete path: straddling, wading,
jumping, and shriek as I catch up
to kiss you, let you go. I see you
steps away; the sound is of a long
corridor. I know the words *I love you,*
now, as a kind of calling.

# Song

Each night I sing songs to pattern her descent
to sleep. They rally, lag, start over, till
she's hushed, shut and absent. She'll forget
every word. But I tell myself their cast's

embedded in her mind like the tenacious,
bony grid of an Etruscan town: steeped
in red earth, metres closer to the planet's
core, silenced by new dirt, tar, a fabricated

higher crust, and on that the imperturbable,
never dreamed of houses; their heedless
windows gulping every cringe and glare of light.

# After the Carnival

We got there too late. Small girls
in lilac wings scuttled to their mothers.
The clouds callused purple. All
heights lit in the coming dark: sea
white where it broke, sky silver-grey,
mauve and plum; *Gigi's* blue-neon
static as memory. I set her free
anyway. The wind began to turn
at its massive root, stirring mini-
tornadoes of cast confetti: pinks
stamped beige, violet and yellow
gone dun in the dusk; it carried and
dangled streamers mid-air. She
was enchanted: clawing at debris,
hurling her broken laugh up
with the tatters, running new metres,
her hair in stuck tufts. The wind
cored my lungs, all words gone. How
to tell the strength and the frailty;
the giddiness of this charge?
The evening was set to rupture – all
disbanded now, into *Gigi's* or cars,
and blankly tracking her play in
the oncoming rain, the swirl of paper;
the cars, villas, in her upturned face,
torn up, wheeling, and lighter than dust.

# II

## THE GLASS EYE

You must be taught to love me. Human beings must be
      taught to love
silence and darkness.

LOUISE GLÜCK

# The Glass Eye
*in the blood pressure clinic*


I pump the black bulb
until the pressure cuff's so tight
I fear the heart could burst –
release.

The rhythm of the pulse is hooves,
the adumbrated pause
as though it sprouted wings,
till again the beat descends.

One man would disclose the velocity
of rain, the play at Lord's
as he buttoned his mac,
reached for his cane.

Today his fingers crabwalk,
unbidden,
to his black eye-patch, lift,
unhook his blue glass eye.

There's the flasher's quelled excitement
in his tenuous smile,
the other eye teased by clinic light,

and the expanse of socket,

large enough to lose a baby's fist;
a dark that drops
so far I think I'll see the brain glisten –
something like a spider's fitful fur –

but nothing. Just the windlessness
of noon eclipse,
talk scattered like scared birds.
In the dying of footsteps, voices,

it's the amplified pause of sex:
thought halted, long
dissolve of seconds, the pupils'
drunken well –

We only wake
the moment he snaps
the eye back in
to corridor-voices,

lights, the bubble-gum pink
of gut diagrams.
He lumbers to the door
like a man from confession

and he'll board the bus
sifting my silence,
my reluctance
to bear witness,

as I busily notate
his blood's music,
usher in the next man,
my lungs abrupt

with small-talk,
and shut my eyes
to the stethoscope again
like a child with a shell.

## Mastectomy

It's an effortful, uneven line
across your chest, a bashed lip
blood's still vacant from:
*Touch it.*

My fingers quiver, though you tell me
*it's* still numb: two more years
till nerves yawn and crackle.
In place of abundant flesh,
there's space and bone. A long,
misjudged step – like missing
a stone stair in the country dark –
and I lose a breath, and all my hands'
bones murmur at the loss.
I rest my palm deep into it,
study your new form, tipped
like a half-loaded boat.
My silence runs and gains;
and that's it. Outside, a brittle

cold unclinches: snow on the Eastern
Plains till, incrementally
and with a hiss of dryness
the world's wiped white. Little
sinkers meandering down,
each their own sailing, selfish,
thoughtless weight, many times
lighter than my hands.

# The Witness

The piano next door
was quick as water,
yet we almost felt the pad
of flesh tapped on ivory.

Irregular scales ascended,
irrevocable as my heart
at night – always nearly
stopping, never quite.

You'd drum out the given
rhythm on the pulled skin
of my sternum,
and I'd write the melody

on your stomach with
my tongue, my heart
declaring a ton of blood
that had me gasp.

My ventricles were drowned,
you said. They swallowed
a double beat that sent
a geyser up the thin

carotid at my throat,
half-closing it.
It was a year of secret
afternoons before we knew

we eavesdropped singing
lessons. Then, after
the deaf hours of sex,
we could distinguish

the faint, silver thread
of voice along a phrase;
the lone soprano's
crescendo surfacing

shakily through the wall.
It was the only presence
ever to impinge on us;
the nearest thing to witness.

We listened hard then –
I held my breath
as I brushed your spine;
you sobered as you lay

your head on me, heeding
the erratic red winces
and lurches of my chest:
so uncontained

they nearly filled me,
and left you cupping
a blood-logged heart,
its laden protestations.

# Photograph

The click is less than a second. I trash
reel after reel, hold you still, stiller:
your bones moan like a boat on a river.
An afternoon won't get you; the flash

beats off you like rain. But give me a polished
museum, a NO PHOTOGRAPHY sign,
a night-watchman's footsteps diminuendo,
you cordoned off, and I'd wear you to bone.

If I could paint, you know I'd catch you
with a deft dab of light in the corner
of the eye. Your expression would hug you
like a slept-in nightdress, like a bulb-drunk moth.

As it is, every moment's unresolved
and cadges, neatly, onto the next one.

## Undone

Stainless prairie light. Gas-station,
blue street sign, so crystalline
they seemed to shake;

your wind-chimes hung
separate as careful bruises.
*I keep forgetting to breathe.*

Sappho located desire, I said,
not in the heart but the lungs'
startled emptiness. You hunched

on the stoop, in shades against
the glare, and met my lips
glassy-eyed with shock. But

my last turn around the street,
(perhaps because we'd never
see each other again) you jumped

and waved as though to a small
plane. Your house receded
in my rear-view mirror

as though tumbling through
water. Silver-chimes blurred
with the suggestion of song.

# Matricide

The confession spilled, soaked in whiskey:
*My God, what have I done?*
His head hit the interview desk.

The ninety-year-old mother lay twisted
on her hearth like a wrecked bicycle,
each capillary of her face caved in;

on her skirt, the son's semen, gleaming
with the awkwardness of truth.
He was deaf to questions,

couldn't untangle his soused tongue.
But when he glimpsed bare-breasted
women on the police station wall

his head reared up. And the constable,
larky at 3 A.M., turned the pages for him,
on tits, lips, arses. His skull lifted

as though by strings, and sank.
Lifted, eyes glazed with booze,
as though the only live synapses

in his short-circuited brain
ignited to this. In his struck
expression you almost heard

the timed click of the gas-ignition,
the furnace's dull roar,
in a dark and sleeping house.

# Her Hands

*Anna Mae Pictou-Aquash, 1945–76*

The day they buried her was cold
enough to crack the skin. Women
pick-axed frozen ground, tongues
cleaving to the white, acid wind.

Officials had hacked off her hands
'for identification'. The young woman
frozen at the curve of a creek
had a bullet lodged in her cheek,

her long hair had grown a breath
longer. Did they bury her, at least,
with her hands folded back in,
as Egyptians wrapped the heat

of guts away from the scooped
woman? She carried tobacco,
beaded jewellery, clothes
with her to the other world,

and perhaps her own lost hands.
I imagine her dismantled bones
now fallen flat to the ground,
starkly describing the girl,

as a disembowelled barrel, magazine
placed at its side, sketches the gun;
as the coyote's found in its puzzle
of femur, vertebrae, and skull.

Each of her fingers fleshless and silent,
phalanges lapsed a bare millimetre
apart; the stars' beasts patterned
and arcing over the Plains.

## NOTE

Anna Mae Pictou-Aquash, American Indian activist and Wounded Knee warrior, was found dead at the bottom of a ravine in Pine Ridge South Dakota, Winter 1976. Officials gave cause of death as exposure and, within days, severed her hands at the wrist and buried the rest of her as Jane Doe. The hands were used for formal identification, but once the body was known to be that of Pictou-Aquash her family insisted on a second autopsy, and cause of death was recorded as a .32 caliber bullet through the back of the skull. She was reburied, under her real name, at Pine Ridge in South Dakota, disinterred twenty-six years later, and buried again in her native Mi'kmaq Land. Only one of her assassins has been convicted. The legal process, and much speculation, continue.

## Mafia Flowers

4 A.M., you're called to the blindness of a country night
where you only tell the mute space of your eyes,
awkward step, formless breath.

The farmhouse is lit: a cage of day. Every lamp
and overhead jammed on, the unshakeable light
of a hundred suns. The white haired man's

vertical in the middle of the room, eyes popped
of meaning like a baked fish. Red hands covering
his mouth in the first fresh jump of shock,

though the florist's van came in daylight, innocent,
at the regular hour of eight. *'Why'd you wait so long
to call?' 'There were more than I'd reckoned.'*

The room's bright as a butcher's shop with blooms.
Not blooms, not flowers. Wrought, dyed, compressed
funeral wreaths. Dense, satin-sashed circles,

and one spelling his name in rusty chrysanths.
It's propped on his straight chair, another's laid
on the bed, another on the sports section

at the folding table, more overwhelm the floor.
Tight daisies in fanciful blue, salmony pink,
hawkish yellow, heaving the scent and stickiness

of God's nature, amassed beyond wonder.
The colours of Gabriel's miraculous, oily wings
(as fleshed out by men). You take your cap off,

bedazzled at the light, at this man's funeral
and the man not dead. You walk the creaking wreaths,
pretending notes, pour grappa to restore his voice,

bag them like bodies, flick switches one by one
to a dim bedside lamp, so as you step out into the cold
the moon reasserts itself calmly on stones,

the natural order of things. But as you drive,
you can't shake the image of the man slunk in his chair
– crazy – refusing to wake his brothers or tell a soul

of this visitation. The daylight and angels and wreaths
are his – whatever crime he may or may not have done –
as if he conjured each flower himself; he stinks of them.

The same as if 14-year-old Mary had gone running
to Elizabeth, broad-sided by her elaborate tale, saying
it was nothing of her idea and she'd as soon forget it.

Too late. Already the gold congeals above her head,
and Elizabeth's eyeing her warily, her flesh
and blood womb leaping in fear.

On the main road the dawn develops, grey
as sanity, the town is a host of cool witnesses
waking, and as you turn into your lane

there's an almighty rightness you're still
clinging to a month on
when news of his death is delivered.

# Annunciation

Slug and loneliness of midday sun. Crack
of shadow: a faunish boy presenting her
a clean white flower. Closer. He shores up
the noon shade till it's night. Compacted must

of feathers, horse-feed. She staggers till
clutched at the giving band of waist – limbs
go limp like puppies taken at the scruff.
His head bows to two arced shoulders. Begins

the blood's coarse trailing like a loaded sweep of wings.
Cicadas hushed. Her reticulated muscles
chafed. Dry spasm. And in her head,
a miniature song of fear: pollen on her pale

dress: brush it and it deepens, stains. Soon
enough he pours, scorched and long as though
he'd saved it up.
                    The dilation of her knowledge
a calm eye, opened. She runs on stunned legs,

hair undone, each blameless feather
woven in the trembling lucidity of sky.
Neck and thighs bruised as though still
held by an invisible god. An excision

in the hot day. *I am chosen.* At Elizabeth's
door her nicked lips sting with a pain
she knows to stifle: the trail of salt,
its ringing insinuation of truth.

## On Saint Gianna (1922-62) who died as a result of refusing essential medical treatment in order to save the life of her unborn child

Coming home to Suffolk it's the winter trees
strike me: gristly and intricate as bisected lungs.
No seething green or plumage. It would take
a teeming heat to burgeon the faith
of Giovanna, the flocks of surrogate angels

I imagine she summoned. I think of her
as I walk into the house, and, on tiptoe,
set a tin on a highest kitchen shelf. So high –
so out of my reach – it almost flips back
and clatters to the floor. I think leaving

a baby must be like that: hoisting him into
the future – away – by the very ends
of your helpless fingertips. Newborns split
from their mothers have no home to turn back to;
the air may always smell of someone else's house.

My own baby's sleeping, though new nightmares
will wake her, their necessary rehearsals of loss.
Outside the trees shape-shift in the slippery dusk;
a ready mind could make out a face. But only mine
appears in the glass, white and pinched as a flame.

# The Banyan Tree

*in memory of my father*


The trunk was a flayed and muscular arm:
each strained tendon imploring the sky,
where dark shoals of leaves sprouted
more leaves, and wagging fingers of black,
beating birds. It engulfed our end of town –
its criss-cross trunks a thick forest of shoots
grown down and hooked into earth;
the girth of its barnet straddling streets,
blasting latitudes of telegraph-wires.
I saw it everywhere: it was my pole-star
as I loped home from town or beach.
It glided like the moon on a night drive.

But it was those first dawns without you
the Banyan became its own. Its ashen
trunks broke the light to me. I watched
the pitch mosaic of leaves paw the heavens
and let myself believe in gods again.
How many fists from the nude strength
of that arm? It took it all: the punch
of yellow sun; the mynahs' crashing song.
The lilac day-moon, lofty and off-centre,
treading its irrelevance.

## November Sunflowers

If I see anything like the swift difficulty
with which you left your body it's this:
row on row of charred and hopeful faces –
a black sea if it weren't for the spaces
between leaves, stems, the grizzled gradations
of the seeds. The green and breathing life
sucked out so clean (like the Egyptians'
trick with hook, and brain) its dumb semblance
is preserved. All these thousand faces tilt
at one angle to a long-gone sun. Like newborns,
open-mouthed, like those who turn as one
to Mecca. Like your white body, unbruised
and over. The shape of waiting when
waiting is, with one sharp frost, removed.

# The Reflex

Then we had to undress the new patient.
We freed her thin arms from her top, passed
her hands from one of ours to the other,

guided her scarred wrists as she pulled
down her jeans. Like suitors we preserved
a fine electricity of contact, and I noted

the slow curves of a 14-year-old girl –
muted waist, bare scoops of breasts;
the drugged grease of her gaze, as though this

new growth were salted for us.
She was malleable. So slack
we could have rolled her in water

like silk and pegged her to dry.
She snaked down the bath-tub
to condensation and sweat; the wet

weed of hair bothering her face,
her hands too doped to connect.
I rested my arms on the side;

the steam rose; her starved pelvis
emerged in a crisp bluish line;
and she dove. She slipped, hard,

through our grasp. We grabbed
water; hit flesh, porcelain; fingered
the newly breathing hair. She threw

her legs high, and as they broke
to the astonishing lightness of air,
she almost wheeled over. Her mind's

one living note riffled the world
for an exit as a prisoner is alert
to any envelope of sun.

But her lungs smarted and wrung
themselves like hands; and her legs,
as we cradled her and the bath

swallowed its load, kicked
like a newborn lamenting
the apparent desertion of gravity.

# After the blood test

she walks to the harbour, where turquoise
and green fishnets lie piled, all
with the cloudy weightlessness of white
hair. Each morning the fishermen sort
them, glasses at the nose's tip,
as a seamstress might shuffle fabric,
or a butcher garner the rebellious guts
of a cow. They stand in threes or fours
in the steady sunshine, all watching
their hands, the heaped nets.
The boats are tethered, slick
from the dawn trip, on the brink
of the cables' clank, the tub-thump
of static collision. She watches them
in the arch discomfort of having
her blood's casket opened, her blackest
secrets sprung. Who doesn't conceal
some rank asymmetry? Adrenaline
shoots from her stomach to fingertips.
She sits very still, as for a photograph.
The fishermen don't see her; they're looking
for rents (though this fine nylon's so strong
it wouldn't rip; so invisible the fish
must ooze in with the current of light).
Or just untangling, preparing
for the saturated bloom, to open
like a parachute under the water.

# The Baptism

*(for the Genung family)*

Out of eye-purpling sun,
the crushed ranks of whistle-blowing pilgrims,

we snuck a right
into a quiet, white courtyard,

through an ordinary door,
and crossed a divide

into St Peter's
vertiginous, dark torso.

The emptiness shocked.
It throbbed like amniotic fluid

with the thousands
of mouths massing outside.

All that moved:
great trunks of flying dust in sunlight,

our private group
padding to the font with sleepy kids

heavy on our chests.
But as they baptised the baby

I could only stare
at Michelangelo's *Pietà*:

heard for the first time,
the vacuum of her speechlessness;

noted her ruffled
head-dress, (as though, she'd raked

her hands through it
hot hours ago); felt the devastated

dead-weight of her legs
giving the wide, low lap; understood

the long arms gathering
the dead son: not *Look what you've done*

but *This is what I have.*
And her right hand invisible but

for the elongated fingers
propping him, like twigs.

As though he'd tumbled
from the sky, like Icarus, that other boy,

but instead of smashing
at the impact of water (that gives,

but not briskly
enough), was caught

in the snagging,
perfect arms of a tree.

# The Ring

It was a pendulum on my bone-light hand,
4 grams, 18 carats, the weight of swollen lips
those first days, blazing new in the salt air
like a cut.

Again, you dreamed your own slid off
your unaccustomed finger.
Stump nerves finding it, forgetting,
prickling at this foreign presence.

We journeyed to where day and night
peeled back: the shade of dirty pearls.
At three thousand metres
our lungs delineated, flinched,

and wind-slanted shrubs pared to black
against tooth-yellow snow.
Marriage changes nothing but the light
in which you cast things. Our last day

in the mountains, the frozen lake
was too immense to hold, gave up
to tilting ice-floes, collapsed
to tessellations – as though jolted

and sliced at all its fault-lines.
I'd almost forgotten the ring:
its weight absorbed into my own;
the gold almost parting

to my fingernail's curiosity.
Its fleshy give, so unlike
our gelid bones, stubbornly
roseate, as though just breathed on.

# Honeymoon in the Midnight Sun

All night our muscles parry
the sea's tug,

but the water in my glass
barely trembles.

3 A.M., the sun's a white bulb
jarring us minute

on minute. On the shore
picnic fires smoke;

kids long herded
to bed, dizzy

with the light's expectation.
These new nights

sing through our curtains
in a lung-less note;

the mind gets thirsty
for endings.

Your brain, high on promises,
has grasped sleep

like a baby's fist.
Alone in these bright waters

I see slivers of land
ignore the sun's

rattled grace and darken
to themselves this one hour,

with the weight of hands
almost resting in a lap.